THE
"S"
WORD

SALES: THE LIFEBLOOD
OF YOUR BUSINESS

A sales book for business owners

BY ROB BEDELL

ISBN: 978-1707916375

First Edition: November, 2019

Book cover design: Dana Paris
Editing: Kirsten Rees | MakeMeASuccess

For information contact:
LinkedIn: https://www.linkedin.com/in/robbedell/

Table of Contents

The "S" Word Workbook: There is a companion book, *The "S" Word Workbook* which I recommend you purchase and can be used alongside this book to take action. However, it is not required in order to read and benefit from this book.

CHAPTER 1

Sales: The Lifeblood of Your Business

Sales! The "S" word. The word sometimes sends fear into people's hearts. Why does it do this? Because most people, business owners included, don't know what sales is. There has been a negative impression of what sales is and with reason. But you have nothing to fear because sales is the lifeblood of your business and it's not hard to understand it once we break everything down.

By the end of this book, you should appreciate sales. You will understand it. You could even grow to enjoy it. If someone is avoiding the "S" word, they don't really understand SALES.

I was originally going to write a sales book for salespeople. I did my research and found out how many books on sales were out there. There were lots for different sales techniques and methods, many of which were good. There are others on the psychology of sales and the mindset. There were also books on closing the sale. There were a lot of different ways I could have gone. But all of this changed when I was doing a webinar showing the effectiveness of having a sales process. It was for business owners, a lot of business owners.

The presentation went well and I had participation the whole time. I explained how having a sales process for everyone to follow will help everyone on the sales team perform at the same, high level. When you have a process, you can see where a salesperson gets stuck and know where they need further training. I also showed when combined with lead scoring, it saves a company time, money, and frustration. By having a sales process, businesses see more sales, more often and faster. As usual, at the end of the presentation, I opened up the channel for questions. That's when it got interesting.

One person started to ask about when they made time for business development. Another asked about when they did customer addition. Finally, I cut in. I said, "You mean sales?" That's when it happened. I could hear all of them groan, ugh! I then asked, why is everyone so afraid of the word, SALES! The "S" word! After all, it is the lifeblood of all businesses.

When I asked what they thought sales was, I got a few of the expected. "It's controlling the conversation," or "It's influencing their decision." I thought it was great they knew of some of the old-school, sales masters, the Zig Ziglar and Dale Carneys. And while it was great, they knew, it wasn't what they needed to know. I explained, if you are selling 6, 7, 8 figure products or services to C level executives, you probably would need to understand those techniques. They are very helpful in those situations, but since most business is not done at that level for small businesses, they didn't need it. And if they try to use those methods on a small business owner, they will probably cut you off and end the sales call.

It's not to say the small business owner (small business = $500,000-$50 million) doesn't understand it. Most of them do and because of this, they will feel you are 'selling' them instead of educating them on how you can help. You need to talk to them, the way you want people to talk to you. Now, doesn't that make a lot of sense?

When I was done with the seminar, I realized what most business owners needed. Granted, some knew a few of the techniques or methods but they didn't have a foundation of sales to build from. They didn't understand what sales meant.

This is what I am doing with this book. Giving business owners a foundation from which they can understand sales. There may be some who don't feel they need to understand sales. They can hire people for this. I get it. Business owners have a lot on their plate. Why add more?

In most of my first meetings with business owners or someone who runs a small business, I ask one question. "If I came into your business in a sales capacity and wanted to blow the doors off of sales, I mean just beat the goal by 20%, 50%, or even 100%, what do I have to do?" A majority of the time, I get a blank stare. I tell them it's ok and explain a lot of business owners don't know. It's why they hire someone to do it, right? But if sales drop, do you know what's wrong and how to fix it?

Sometimes, I get a simple response like, "You just go out and sell". When I ask what that means, they usually don't know. Other times, they say "go out and explain why they need your offering". I tell them, this is only part of it. Then they ask for my definition. A lot of it will seem like common sense. Then I introduce them to one of my sayings. The base of sales, the boiled down simplest explanation is this.

"Sales is simply starting a productive conversation." - Rob Bedell

Don't get me wrong, a lot of the techniques and methods are great. They work when used in the right setting. But if you don't have a foundation of sales from which to build, most of it won't sink in and therefore will not be effective. It's like trying to drive around town without putting gas in your car. You might get to one meeting but not the next one! Yes, you may get results but they could be even better if you have everything you need.

Again, is there more to sales? Yes! And while it may be helpful as a business owner or someone who runs a business to understand different sales techniques and methods, if you don't want to invest the time to learn everything, you will at least have a basic understanding of sales when you finish this book.

When common sense becomes common practice, this is when you find success. The "S" Word, sales is the lifeblood of your business, so you need to have an understanding of it.

CHAPTER 2

What is Sales?

Sales tactics have been around for centuries, going back to the old west, there were the snake oil salespeople. There are sayings like, "If you believe that, I have beachfront property in Colorado to sell you." This is not sales. There are con people out there and they are at every level. It could be some person on the corner offering fake tickets to a show or a person in a suit offering a real estate deal with a name and no plan. Yes, there are bad people in the sales industry It's the case with any industry. Even so, for every bad person in each industry, there are many more who are great.

There are doctors traveling the world healing people for free. We have lawyers doing pro-bono work for people in need of help. There are cops volunteering off duty to help keep the peace. And yes, there are a lot of salespeople doing a great job and helping people and companies avoid bad things and enjoy the good things in life and business. So, keep this in mind when thinking of sales.

"SALE is a four-letter word, it's why every person should focus on SALES." - Rob Bedell

This is not to say a sale should not be celebrated and congratulated. Some should, but make sure it doesn't distract from the rest which should come too. At times, a salesperson may get caught up in the one big sale they got. It took a long time. They did a lot of work. And if the sales cycle from the initial contact to the close of the sale is long, it may be a while before they get the next one. So, it's good to celebrate the big one, but it's also powerful to use the momentum and what you learned from it to get the next sale and the next and the next. Now you have sales.

Now, we have a better mindset about sales. It is the lifeblood of most businesses. We understand it's ok to celebrate the big one but not to get stuck on it. Rather, use the momentum and what was learned to get more. But we still haven't defined what sales is. The basic foundation of sales is simple. Sales is simply starting a conversation with a purpose.

I'm sure a lot of people are saying, "there has to be more to it." Yes, there is, but the start of it is simply starting a conversation, in person, over the phone, in an email, text, or whatever platform you work from. To get sales, you need to start conversations. Now you may be thinking, well, everyone can do that. Everyone can start a conversation, right? Well, some struggle and a few don't believe they can but you can overcome this. Here's what I've learned:

Before you think you have to be an extrovert to be in sales, let me make sure you understand that is not true. It's usually easier but introverts can as well. There is a part of the introvert group who just don't like talking to people at all. I know people like this. I have friends like this. They are not in sales. A person has to be able to and even more so, want to start a conversation to be in sales.

Can a marketing piece close sales without "talking" to people? I guess it depends on your definition of talking to someone. I say marketing pieces do talk to people. Most of the time, a person needs to be involved to close sales.

Also, I said 'conversation'. I didn't say lecture. I didn't say preach. A conversation is an exchange of idea(s) between two or more people. I always focus salespeople on the word 'exchange'. It needs to be at least two-sided. This leads into another saying I use. Sales is like the human body: two ears, one mouth. Listen twice as much as you talk. I'll go more into this topic later.

Some may be thinking, an exchange doesn't happen when people read a script. That is true. I don't like scripts. It is not to say they don't work at all. Some scripts do, but not if you want to build a relationship and have continued business. They can work if it is a one-time sale. But a lot of times, those can be sketchy. That is when sales is a four-letter word. I'm not saying they are all that way, but from my experience, a lot of them are.

I do like having talking points for salespeople. There are certain topics which should be discussed in the sales conversation. We'll go into more of them in chapters that follow. Having talking points help open up the conversation and if a salesperson gets stuck, they can always fall back to one of the talking points.

We get it now, right? Sales isn't a bad word. It's the lifeblood of most businesses. Sales is a good thing most of the time. Sales is starting an effective conversation. Conversations are not bad things. A conversation is an exchange of ideas between at least two parties. It's not one-sided. We all now get the 10,000-foot level of what Sales is!

What should be in the conversation? Do you, the person who runs the business, know why people or companies should do business with you? Do you know your value proposition? Sales is simply starting a conversation and when this common sense becomes common practice, this is when you find success.

CHAPTER 3

What is Your Value Proposition?

As a business owner, or someone who runs a small business, you know your business: what it is and how it works. You know how great your business is. But do you, and everyone who works for you, know your value proposition? It's a fancy way of saying, why should people work with you?

What problem do you solve? What benefit do people or companies get from working with your business? It sounds like a simple question which should be easy to answer, but more often than not, I find most people at a company don't know this.

If your business offers a service, why is it better than your competition?

If you run a restaurant, why should I come to your place as opposed to the place down the street?

What makes your product/service better than their product/service?

If your mind immediately said, "We're cheaper." you better find some other reasons. Some company will come along to find a cheaper way of offering what you have. Basing everything on price may work for a while, but when a problem comes up, people will say it's because you're so cheap. Having a fair price is important, however, it should not be your only reason.

When working with an insurance inspection company, I helped them grow from regional to national, growing 400% over eight years. I was able to do this because they had the best product on the market at the time. They were not the cheapest. So, I used that to our advantage - what can you use to yours that you're not already?

I would go into insurance companies and say, "You can always find a company that will do it for five or ten dollars cheaper, but when a problem arises, as they always do with business, we have the best customer service.

In this case, it was a father-son team and they believed their customers wanted, "Time service and quality". Yet, their clients were saying something different. "When a problem happens, as they do, we know we can call them. They find out what happened and tell us what they will do to make sure it doesn't happen again."

So, we changed the value proposition. When we lead with customer service and communication, it changed everything. Companies tried us out and found it was true. Even when it didn't have an immediate impact, when problems came up with the cheaper company, they thought of us and called.

By focusing internally, on customer service and communication, we were able to satisfy our clients. Thinking you know your value proposition doesn't make it the case. So, how do you find it? Ask your customers. Ask them why they work with you. What they tell you helps create your value proposition.

Once you find your value proposition, you need to make sure everyone at your company knows it and talks about it. They should talk about it both externally to customers and prospects and internally to ensure everyone has the same understanding of it. You may be asking why someone who doesn't talk to customers would need to know it. It's because it creates a mindset. And when everyone at a company has the same, successful mindset, they do better.

Do you want to have a better work environment? Make sure everyone is on the same page with what your company offers and understands the value of what you offer. In order for that to happen, you, the person running the business needs to understand it and able to explain it to your team. If you also have *The "S" Word Workbook*, you will find a page to write out your value proposition to share with your team.

I encourage you to talk to your salespeople and ask why people should work with your business. If they stumble on explaining it, you'll know if it's either nerves because now the top boss is asking or they don't know how to explain it.

If they don't have their elevator pitch down and can't spit it out at any time to anyone, you will know that some training needs to happen for them. If they can't do it at all, you then know a lot more training is needed. I also encourage business owners to ask the same thing of whoever is running the sales team if it's not them: why should people do business with us?

Do you have a sales director/manager? Can they answer the question without pause? They may have mental fatigue, or have what's called a brain-fart sometimes, but if it happens every time, do you have the right person running your sales team?

Does your marketing reflect your value proposition? If you outsource your marketing, does the company you work with know it? Remember, you want your whole team and everyone who works with your company to know it. There is a section in *The "S" Word Workbook* where you can note the main companies you compete with and what things make you stand out.

I'll end this with another saying. One voice in a crowd may not be heard, but when a company speaks together, it creates a roar. Make sure everyone knows your value proposition. Make your company ROAR!

Although this may sound like common sense for everyone at your company to know your company's value proposition, when common sense becomes common practice, that's when you find real success.

CHAPTER 4

Do You Know Your Sales Process?

I have over thirty years in sales. If you would have told me when I was in college, I would have a long, successful career in sales, I would have told you, you were wrong. I didn't want to be in sales! I didn't want to talk people into buying something they don't want or need. That's what I thought sales was when I was young.

It's not what sales is and I know this now. At least, now with the internet, public reviews, and forums, those companies don't stay in business too long because selling what doesn't work or people don't need gets exposed online.

But there still is a problem most people starting in sales have even with a solid product or service. I know I had this problem. Granted, I was good with talking with people so I had a natural leg up in sales. Nonetheless, I didn't understand I had a sales process when I started.

Most of the people who do well in sales have a process, whether they know it or not. Until someone told me about how the sales process works, I didn't know I had one. Once I was aware of it, it was obvious. I approached sales in a certain way.

When I started, the internet did not exist. I found my leads by using phone books, newspapers, flyers, commercials on TV, and radio. I found the ones with strong potential and kept going to that well for more leads. I stopped taking them from lead sources that weren't closing. After calling and asking who was responsible for what I had to sell, I would get a name and ask for them then try calling at different times.

Then the internet came and email. If there was no connection within three attempts, I asked for an email and wrote to let them know I was going to come by on a certain day, in a certain timeframe or if that didn't work, to let me know. This got me in contact with the decision-maker.

If I ended up speaking to them on the phone first, I had my list of talking points and questions to get them to talk. Start by making sure it is a good time to talk. Many people think as soon as you get someone on the phone, you just start talking. That can work against you if it's bad timing. By asking if it's a good time to talk, you are showing respect for their time and instantly puts you in a better light starting out.

Regardless of the outcome of the phone call, I would always thank them for their time and schedule a time to follow up. If it was a company I knew would benefit from what I had, I sent treats, cookies, bagels, snacks with my name and my company's name. When I called back, they remembered.me

If I got a meeting, I took snacks, not just for the person but the whole office. Starting with a short introduction of myself and my company, I led into prepared questions which got them talking. Focus on the person and not just the sale. It was all about building the relationship first and sales came from solid relationships.

Again, regardless of the results of the meeting, I would thank them for their time and say goodbye to others as I left, making sure everyone knew there were snacks available for them. The next day, I would send an email thanking them for their time, recap our meeting, and schedule next contact.

There are other steps I take in the sales process to get through the meeting, but this gives you the general idea of the process working for me. In case you're wondering if one sales process works for every business, the answer is no. You build your sales process based on your company, your industry, and your sales cycle. I could write another book on the sales process and mistakes a lot of businesses make. For one, why do you have a sales presentation as a stage? If you can get the sale without doing a long, drawn-out presentation (the 5th one they saw today) would you?

One basic process you can start with is as follows:

Qualify - Do they need what you have? Can you give them what they need? Are they ready to incorporate what you have? This means, if what you have would add 30% new business to them, can they process that business. Are you ready to handle their business? Same thing in reverse.

Educate - This goes two ways. Starting with your education. What are their main needs? What problems do they have which you can solve? Can you show them how you can help them? Will this be mutually beneficial?

Propose - Do you both agree on what is needed on both sides for this to be successful. Get a verbal agreement you see it is mutually beneficial. Many people skip this step and it comes back to bite them when they start working together. The client may not fully understand what is needed on their side. Time to learn. Time to train. People that are needed on their side. People needed on your side.

Contract - This goes into the details about the new relationship. What each side will give and what each side will get.

Advocacy - What needs to happen after the sale? Who needs to be involved and introduced to the new arrangement. Regular follow up to ensure it is working. This is another step a lot of businesses forget and this results in losing clients.

> *"Do it when you have to, not when YOU feel*
> *YOU need to." - Rob Bedell*

If you are new to sales, or even if you have been in sales for a while, does your company have a sales process? If not, you need to create one.

If you do and it's not working well, then learn to tweak it. Even if you have one and it's working, are there ways to improve what you have?

With advances in technology, your process may be able to be improved. Review it at least yearly. Right now, set a reminder for one year to review this - take action which will have an impact. To get a handle on doing this well, there are some questions in the workbook. With the right sales process, you will build more relationships and close more business. Put a good sales process into practice - it gets you more money, more often and faster.

CHAPTER 5

Who is Your Ideal Customer? Where Do You Fit in Your Industry?

A question I always ask business owners is who is your ideal client? Sometimes they say, everyone. Then I have the fun task of letting them know they are wrong. Regardless of what you think, not everyone would want or will use what you have regardless of how great it is. Everyone is not your target market.

If you don't know who your ideal client is, you won't know where to find them or how to talk to them when you do find them. Most small businesses have smaller marketing budgets if they have one at all, so if they don't know who they want to talk to, that small budget will be wasted. A lot of business owners don't see the value in marketing because they haven't seen the return on their marketing dollars. It makes sense. Conversely, when they target their message to a more specific audience, they get better results. Even Coca Cola wouldn't try to market their original recipe to people into health. Every small business should follow that lead and focus their marketing specifically on their ideal clients.

How do you find your ideal customer? If you've been in business for a while, look at your current customer base. Which ones are most profitable? Which are the easiest to work with? It's important to not just look at the numbers on the books because it doesn't give you the whole answer. If you have a client who spends a lot with you yet takes up a lot of time and resources, they may not be profitable.

One company I worked with, had a client who paid more than most of the other clients. The only problem is how much time the whole team spent working on their work. They wanted custom reports. They wanted a different format than the norm. They wanted more work done on each case that we worked on. The people who worked on the cases for us, wanted more money to do them. So, if we just looked at the money they spent with us, it looks like a great account. After looking at all of the other resources they ate up, we realized they weren't the most profitable, ideal client.

We found the smaller accounts, using our reports, our format and the average amount of work done for each case were more profitable. While the larger account was good to have by name, the smaller accounts were more ideal. Plus, they were easier to get into and get set up. They took a lot less on the backend, having less of an effect on the bottom line. If you have someone running your accounting, ask them which clients are the most profitable. If you run your own books, look at everything affecting the bottom line and ask everyone who has contact with them how much time they spend working with them.

Once you know who you are trying to reach, make sure you understand where you stand in your industry. Some of this should come from your value proposition, but it also comes from the competition. What do you do better? Where are they strong?

Are you the lowest price? Are you the best quality? Do you have the best customer service? The answer to the last question should always be yes. Regardless of where you fit in the industry, if you have great customer service, you will retain your customers much longer than when you don't. The importance of good customer service could be a topic for another book. For right now, understand that every company I worked with leading their industry, has great customer service. If you also have *The "S" Word Workbook*, flip to the section on ideal customers and work on this.

You won't get everyone and you'll go nuts trying. Don't try to have everyone as a customer, it's common sense and again when this becomes common practice, that's when you find success.

CHAPTER 6

Some Leads Suck

A lot of managers/business owners think all leads are good, meaning they could lead to a sale. This is not the case. Bad leads are EVIL and can kill your business. What do I mean by that?

The fastest way to burn out your sales team is to give them a bunch of unqualified, bad leads. These are leads which have not been qualified, i.e. do they need what you have and is the contact information correct. Buying a list of unqualified leads and handing it to your sales team will lead to unproductive and unhappy salespeople.

How do you get qualified leads? If your marketing is set up correctly, you can vet leads coming in through it. By using video marketing with a squeeze page, you can capture information which helps with this. Work with your marketing team to let them know what qualifies as a good lead, who is your ideal customer, etc. If you don't have a marketing team and have a list, have an assistant go through and qualify it.

You should score all leads coming in. You can set up a complex scoring system, or a really simple one. A sample of a simple one would be as follows:

Do they need what you have? +20%

Is the contact information correct? +20%

Can you get them on the phone +20%

Can you get a meeting? +20%

Did it close? +20%

If a majority of the leads don't get more than a 40% score, stop using that source or change the marketing campaign. It is very important for you to have this communication with your marketing. If the marketing team doesn't know what's working and what isn't, they can't fix what they are doing.

Plus, when you score the leads, you can also see where the sales team needs help. If they are getting meetings but not closing a lot, more training may be needed. If qualified leads are not being reached by phone, try email or other means of contact, even a cold drop by. Trying different times of the day can make a difference too.

The best way to find good qualified leads is to look for leads containing most of the elements of your ideal client. Check out the section on lead scoring in the workbook. Yes, in a perfect world a list of only your ideal clients would exist but you're not going to find a list only containing them.

Still, if most of them contain the same elements of those clients, even the ones which aren't ideal, will be profitable. Now, you're handing off partially qualified leads to your sales team and won't waste their time and your money and can keep them from burning out by calling random, completely unqualified leads. Does this make sense? Common sense? More leads does not mean more sales.

CHAPTER 7

Your Company Representation: How to Dress and Talk

With the title to this chapter, you may think of the physical look of your business or what you offer. However, I'm talking about how the people representing your company look to prospects/clients.

Does everyone wear a uniform? Do they all wear professional clothing, i.e. suits, etc.? Or is your company more business casual? How do those who represent you appear? A lot of people think we should dress professionally when out of the office for meetings but this is not always the case in today's business world. In some industries and areas of the country, you would wear a suit, or similar. A lot of people working in finance, especially back east, do wear suits to work every day. But if you are visiting a marketing company in Seattle, by wearing one you could alienate yourself and your message can get lost by your appearance.

Granted, how you want your company to appear is up to you. Take a look externally first and see how your clients appear. If they are jeans and t-shirt, you are business casual. If they are business casual, you are business attire. But when you get to business attire or suits, you don't have to go in one step above. Showing up in a tux wouldn't help.

"I always say to dress one level up from how they dress, so you can stand-out but not alienate yourself."
- Rob Bedell

Many people would say it doesn't matter and just be careful and wear a suit. If you don't know how their staff dresses, you are safer going in dressed business attire. You can adjust it - if you see they are all in jeans and flip-flops, you can say you just came from another client where they dress in suits. Then if appropriate, take off the jacket or loosen your tie.

The important part is consistency with everyone seeing your people. I know some people may just have an inside sales team, so what then? I always say, business casual is good and maybe a casual Friday. How people interact with others, even over the phone, can change with how they dress. So you want inside sales teams to be comfortable, while still feeling like they are at work and not sitting at home in their sweats. There are some good questions in the workbook which may give you insight into how your company is represented.

If you have company shirts everyone wears, then you will have consistency. Is a company uniform needed? Probably not for a lot of small businesses. You have to find a level that you, the person running the business, are comfortable with and fits your industry. This isn't rocket science but things a lot of business owners don't think about. When they do, they realize it's common sense. Make your company stand out but do not alienate your customers.

CHAPTER 8

Coach, Don't Manage People

All of the topics covered in this book are important. I wouldn't waste your time with something that is not. But if no other chapter registers with you, I hope this one does. Because once you understand this, you will get the most out of the people you have on your sales team, even the ones who shouldn't be on your team.

I've seen many books on how to manage salespeople. Some of them have great ideas, but the reason I think they can be improved is if every business owner understood this idea. You manage the sales process, the budget, the policies and procedures but are you coaching the people?

Some may say it's the same thing but it's not. It's a different mindset. A manager wants to get to the number they need. A coach wants to get the best out of each person on their team. When the latter happens, the numbers will be there and a lot of time, more than what was budgeted.

Manager: manages everyone one the same.

Coach: treats everyone fairly but not the same.

Manager: yells at salespeople on the sales floor and rarely recognizes when people do good.

Coach: may snap at someone and question them on the sales floor but gets down to the details in private. They also praise each salesperson in public, making sure everyone knows what is expected and that they will get recognition.

Manager: has a department where people show up and do their job to make sure they don't get fired. The team doesn't want to do more work than they have to. Why should they?

Coach: has a team who understand each of their roles and why they are important to the team. They will work harder and often stay longer to get to where the team needs to go.

Manager: usually points at the salespeople, blaming their efforts when things don't work or the numbers aren't where they need to be.

Coach: takes blame and works with each teammate on how to improve.

When the sales team hit or exceed the numbers, a manager takes credit and may congratulate one or two people. Some salespeople walk away feeling like their efforts don't matter. A coach gives credit to the team and reminds them, 'this is what we get when we work together'. Everyone walks away feeling like they contributed and can't wait to do it again.

Now, your star player may be treated a little different. They may be given a little more freedom, as long as they are hitting their numbers. A newbie will have more hands-on attention until they get down what they need to do. They get more and different coaching.

When I came back to Los Angeles with New Times, we bought two competing newspapers, the Los Angeles View and the Reader and merged them. It was a challenging time for me. I had to sort through accounts, some of which advertised in both papers and decide who got what and make it fair. We got two competing teams to work as one with one common goal, however, I had to figure out the players I had and what role they played on the team.

After a few weeks, I figured out who were teammates and understood their common goal and the ones just in it for themselves. Making cuts is one of the hardest parts, but when you do it the right way, most everyone comes out better.

So I had my team, now it was time to see them work together. I explained what was expected of each and why it was important to the team. They each said they could do what was expected of them, so now it was time to see. As the saying goes, "It looked good on paper."

Tuesday nights were our deadline. Our goal for the week was $26,000. At the beginning of the day, we were at a little over $20,000. It was going to be a lot of work to get to our goal. By 4 pm, we were at $24,000. Everyone was hustling, including myself. I heard people trying to upsell and offer additional parts to sell - the team was working hard.

At 5:30, we were at $25,200. Everyone was banging the phones, calling everyone they could. They called old customers, did cold calls, calling everyone they could. At 6 pm, we were at $25,800.

Gathering the team, I told them they did a good job and I knew how hard they all worked. Then one of the senior salespeople stood up and asked if they could stay later. It caused a ripple effect as everyone jumped up and said they were in.

The production department agreed to push back the deadline. I ran to the accounting department and asked for an extension. They looked at me the way accounting people look at salespeople when they ask for more but gave us another thirty minutes.

In five minutes, we got a $150 ad. We were so close. In the next five minutes, one of the rookies closed a $100 ad. We were above goal. Everyone jumped out of their chairs and gave high-fives. We closed out and everyone walked out wearing huge smiles.

The publisher walked out of her office and asked what was going on. When I told her what happened, she asked if they all volunteered to do overtime. I said yes. She looked around then said, "It looks like you have your team."

So, I'll leave you with one question, which will hopefully get you to understand this chapter fully. Do you just have a sales department, or do you have a sales team? Manage the numbers and the process but coach the people.

CHAPTER 9

Mindset and Sales

I have heard business owners tell their salespeople, "Just get out and sell!" When I ask them what this means, a lot of time they get bothered and say, "You know, just go sell." I always try not to push them too hard because at this time, I know they are frustrated with their sales team.

'Just go out and sell' isn't always the best way to get what you want out of your sales team, especially if you don't know what it means. What if you changed it to, "Hey, just go out and talk with people. Go have a conversation and find out what their problems are and see if what we have can benefit them. If so, tell them how we can benefit them. If they still say no, ask if they know any other businesses who could use our help."

Doesn't that sound much clearer as to what you are asking them to do? Plus, it will change the mindset of your sales team. When you give clear direction, they will understand what they need to do. Mindset is extremely important for salespeople.

One of the biggest issues I see in a lot of small businesses I have worked with, is the sales team not being clear as to what they need to do...and why! I know, if they are in sales, they should know why they need to sell. Now, I will put on my old sales training hat and use it for you.

Salespeople should be going out and having conversations with prospects. They should ask questions to see if the prospect has a need you can help with. Continuing the conversation, they can share what your company has and how it can help them with their need. They need to show the benefit of working with your company. That's the foundation of what they need to be doing.

Why do you need to know this? Are you sitting down? Your employees are your customers. When business owners treat their employees like their customers, their employees will do better. The company will do better.

As I said before, treat your sales team all fairly, but not the same. What do they value? What motivates them? Does it fit with your company's goals? If so, great!!

Everyone may not be a good fit, so keep this in mind. And just like customers who really don't fit your ideal customer, likewise you may find at a point, you shouldn't work with certain employees.

Are you shocked? You shouldn't work with every potential customer and you shouldn't employ every person coming in for an interview. If a prospect doesn't see the value in what you offer, you may not want to work with them. If one of your salespeople can't see and understand the value in what you offer, don't employ them. Believe it or not, it may be better for them not to work there, as well.

When I was first promoted to sales manager at New Times, I hired a lady who did great, right out of the gate. She was killing it. I thought it was a great hire on my part and walked around with pride!

Then everything changed, by the fourth month, her numbers were flat. My offer of some extra training or marketing materials were rejected, she was fine. The next month went by and it was the same. After another unproductive month, I pulled her into my office.

I asked was there something personal going on. I didn't need details but wanted to know what happened. She blew the door off the first few months, so I knew she could do this. Then I said, if I needed to make a cut, she would be one of the ones I'd consider. I told her I can give her all of the tools and training she needed to be successful, but I couldn't give her the drive to want to do this. It had to come from her. She said she'd fix it.

The next month, she was back on track, killing her numbers. However, the following month she walked into my office and shut the door. She quit. When I asked her why, she told me what I said really registered. She knew she could do sales but she really didn't want to. She wanted to do marketing and she found a job she wanted. She thanked me, gave me two-week notice, and walked back to her desk.

Now, this is not to say every time a salesperson goes into a slump, you should try to talk them into quitting, no, a slump will happen to even the best salespeople. Sometimes, they get stuck in their heads and can't find a way out. But when it happens, you need to find out why.

First, you need to find out if they want to be there. Ask them to consider if it's what they want to do as a career. If not, then come to an agreement on an exit strategy which works for both of you. Next, if they do want to stay, that's when you need to change their mindset again and go back to the basics: "Just go out and have conversations with prospects. Ask questions to see if they need what we have and if we'd be better than what they have. If so, continue the conversation telling them the benefits of what we have. Will you get everyone? No, but then ask them if they know anyone who would benefit from what you have. Then go and have a conversation with the next person."

Sounds simple, doesn't it. It is. Are there other more complicated ways to do it so you sound really smart and impressive? Maybe but when you break it down to simple steps everyone can do, then you get better results. Everyone will feel more confident they can do that. It puts them in the right mindset to succeed. Succeed for themselves and for the company. Be here and now before you start.

CHAPTER 10

Types of Salespeople, Don't Let Your Star Kill Your Business

I've worked with many sales teams. The teams usually break down as follows:

'Star' salespeople - these are your top performers. They know your offering, how to present it, and how to start a conversation to get the sale. They may even show up early and stay late.

'Bread and butter' salespeople - they know your offering and how to present it. They show up on time and leave on time. You know what you're going to get from them and they are easy to deal with.

'Let's see how this ends up' salespeople - they may be right out of school or have little to no experience. They may work out, or they may not, you just don't know yet.

In all honesty, you need this mix of people to have a solid, productive sales team. If you have all 'let's see' people, it's a lot of work to manage. If you have all 'bread and butter people', it's hard to reach new goals. And if you have all star salespeople, while you might think this would be good, it creates a lot of internal conflict. However, where I've seen the most problems is when the department only has one 'star'.

In situations like this, I've seen more often than not, the 'star' runs the department. I ran into this early in my career when I worked briefly, at a financial newspaper. I started and as I normally do, introduced myself to everyone there. When I introduced myself to a lady, I'll call her Miss AllAboutMe (her name did not fit her), she quickly turned her nose up at me, turned around and ignored me. I didn't think much of it and thought she may be having a bad day.

After a week, I realized Miss AllAboutMe's bad day, was every day albeit she seemed to bring in a lot of business. I was working a lead one day and about to close, when she noticed what I was working on and said, "That's mine." I asked her why she thought that and she told me, they ran with her before many years ago. I asked how long ago and she said it didn't matter and to give it to her.

I went to the manager and explained the situation. He said to give it to Miss AllAboutMe. I asked for a reason since, she had not been in contact with them for a long time, as they did not know who she was or who we were. It should be my account. He then looked at me and said, "You expect me to side with you? Miss AllAboutMe has been here longer and brings in more than you." I replied, "Well, of course, she brings in more than everyone else because she takes what others have worked for. That's not fair." He again looked at me and said, "I'm not going to side with you. Give it to her."

I saw them talking a bit later and laughing. One of the other salespeople came up to me and said. "That's what always happens. Miss AllAboutMe takes everything." I promptly quit. I realized their star salesperson was killing the rest of the staff's chances. And I would not set myself up for failure.

But many sales departments are set up for failure. A lot of times, business owners feel they can't lose a certain salesperson because they bring in so much. While relationships with all clients is important, if you have a solid product or service you will keep the business. Plus, if a business has a couple of larger clients, the business owner/sales leader, should have a relationship with them. If not, it can cause a problem when the star salesperson leaves. If you don't pay attention to your clients, if you let the Miss AllAboutMe-types kill your sales team, it will come back to you, and not in a good way.

You may think in the end, Miss AllAboutMe won because she got what she wanted and I quit. Well, this is when "sales karma" kicks in. A few months later, I was a sales manager at a local newspaper. After one of our manager's meetings, some managers from another department said they finally found a good person they were about to hire. I asked about them. They said her name was Miss AllAboutMe. I stopped in my tracks. I told them, if they hire her, it would destroy the rest of their department. It may not happen immediately, nevertheless over time it would happen and I explained the story of how I knew her.

They were wide-eyed. They said they didn't know what to do because she knew they were going to offer her the job. I said I'd meet them in the lobby and I went down the back way.

When I walked in, I pretended not to notice her as I walked through the lobby. I said 'hi' to the other managers. Then I looked at her, cocked my head and said, "Oh, hi. How are you?" Then I turned and told my colleagues I would see them in the next managers' meeting and walked away.

What I was told was Miss AllAboutMe, didn't speak for the first five minutes of their meeting. When she finally did, she asked if she would ever have to report to me. They said I was a good manager and it may happen. She got up, shook hands, and left. They never heard back from her. So while we may have lost out on a star salesperson, we also avoided a person who might have destroyed the rest of the team, losing more money.

Again, the best sales model has a bit of all types of salespeople. Only stars creates a lot of infighting and no development of your clients. All bread and butter and your business may not grow the way you want it to grow. If you have a small sales team, you probably want some with a mix of both. As the saying for investing goes, don't put all of your eggs in one basket, the same applies with your sales team. Makes sense? Your best group is a mixture of different types of salespeople and it is important they are all treated fairly, but not the same.

Chapter 11

Sales is Like the Human Body: Two Ears, One Mouth.

We've already talked about sales being simply starting a great conversation. We already know a conversation is an exchange of idea(s) between two or more people. It's about asking questions to start that exchange. But here is a key to understanding what this means. Sales is like the human body: two ears, one mouth. Ask your questions then, SHUT UP!

This sounds like a simple thing to do, although it's harder than you think, especially for some people. This is especially hard for people with large egos. They want to share what they have to say. They want everyone to listen to them. They want to 'control the conversation' and think it will result in sales because if they say "buy" everyone should jump and do it. This can work, yet again it doesn't establish the long-lasting relationships you want.

If someone is bullied into buying something, the next few days after, they'll think about it and it will bother them. If what you have works perfectly, then they will think it wasn't the way they wanted, but it's working, so they'll leave it alone... until something happens.

In business 'something' always happens. There are always hick-ups or delays or problems. When these things happen and you bulldozered over someone to get the sale, they may regret it and now there is a problem. So now, you have to work much harder to keep the account.

Early in my career when I was restructuring the classified department for a local weekly newspaper, I had some good salespeople.

I had one who was very aggressive with their sales approach. They would tell the results other advertisers got and imply they would get the same results. I spoke with them in a weekly meeting and told them they had to be very careful in comparing results one client gets and letting other advertisers think they'll get the same results.

I told them it was better to ask the prospect questions, ask what they were looking to get from their advertising and then listen to what they say. I told them, listen twice as much as you talk. I explained when they do this, they may find what they are looking to get from what they do with us, is something that we can't deliver. They said they got it.

The next week, they ended up selling to a high-end contractor who built homes. When I saw it come in, I asked the salesperson about it. Our market did cover some of the higher end of Santa Monica, but I would think this is a longer buying decision. Did he understand it may take a while before he sees anything? The sales rep said he did.

Two weeks later, the salesperson walks into my office and said the contractor was upset as they hadn't gotten any calls and he wanted to talk to me. I told the rep to tell him I'd call him by the end of the day.

I looked at the ad. It was about a complete rebuild of a home focused on new home buyers wanting to do a complete rebuild. It looked like it was geared towards people who flipped homes. I asked for his advertising agreement and it was for a year. I called the salesperson into my office and asked what questions he asked and what they said.

The salesperson said the client wanted to be near people buying new homes and if we had a good real estate section. The rep just sat there after the statement. I asked what they said and I could tell they were nervous. They told him we had a section covering all of the city, even the high-end places above Wilshire. I said, "So you gave him unrealistic expectations?" The rep just shrugged to which I said we'd be discussing this more after the call.

I called the client and he was mad. I let him talk. He was told we had a good real estate section which covered Santa Monica, so he figured he would find people flipping houses. He hadn't gotten one call from it. I let him go on longer until he calmed down. Then I asked him a question, "Do you work with other weekly newspapers reaching a lot of people flipping houses?" There was a long silence.

"No," he eventually said. I asked how long he has been working with people flipping houses. He said he didn't but he wanted to start doing it. I explained how we don't really reach that market and from what I know of it from friends working in the house flipping world, local community newspapers weren't their main resource. I explained we do reach homeowners who may be looking to remodel parts of their home, would this be something he would do? He said yes.

We ended up rewriting his advertising to focus on that part of his business. We did bump up his ad to help with the miscommunication. He seemed happy with this. I checked back with him a month later and he got four calls, one of which he had already booked for a bathroom remodel. More importantly, he was happy.

The conversation I had with the salesperson was firm and to the point. I asked them if they understood why the client was upset. They said yes. I asked if they now understood why to ask questions, listen, and respond based on what they said. They said yes. I asked if they understood why they were not getting paid commission on the ad for the next month. They were upset but eventually said yes.

They learned from that situation and so did I. They learned to ask questions, listen, and then see if we had something they could use. They learned how to ask more questions from what the prospect said, i.e. looking for people to flip houses, to people looking to refurbish a bathroom and lead them to what we had.

I learned to ask my sales team what they asked prospects and what the response to the question was. If they asked the question, yet couldn't tell me what they said in return, I knew they weren't making sales like the human body with two ears and one mouth. I then reminded them of that idea and told them to try again. Make the idea common sense for them. Listen more than you talk.

CHAPTER 12

Celebrate Success in Public, Discipline in Private

I think one of the biggest problems business owners/sales managers have is how, when, and where to celebrate successes and handle disciplinary actions. What do you do on the sales floor? What do you cover in sales meetings? What do you discuss in private?

Now, some people may say what I cover in this chapter is common sense. I'll go back to my saying, "When common sense becomes common practice, that's when you'll find success." But there are a lot of people who don't handle this right and when done the wrong way, in the wrong place and at the wrong time, it can cause more problems than it solves.

One of the biggest mistakes a lot of green, rookie "managers" make is they focus on correcting what is wrong before celebrating what is right. It's not entirely their fault. A lot of times senior management, or ownership, focuses on that too. "Make sure they don't say this." "Make sure they don't do that." These are things said to them, so they focused on the bad things to avoid. It's what "managers" do.

Switching back to the coaching approach, let's start with focusing on the good things. I forget where I first heard this notion, it's one we should all pay attention to a bit more: "You hit/get what you focus on." When you're driving down the road and are focused on the tree. You're more likely to hit the tree. When you are focused on the road and avoiding other cars, you'll have a smooth drive home.

Now we know what we should start with, the good stuff. You'll notice I started out by saying "celebrate successes". So, let's start there. How do you celebrate successes? My first instinct would be to celebrate loudly, everywhere, and often - until I took a step back. Some people don't like to be put in the spotlight, even when it's good. So how you celebrate depends on the salesperson who had their success.

If you have a type-A salesperson, yes, celebrate it in front of everyone. You can start with an email to them, saying "good job" depending on your organization and its policies. You can do it on the sales floor, making sure everyone can hear. You can repeat it in a sales meeting. Type-A people like to be recognized.

If you have someone who is shy and likes to work in the shadows, you can still start with an email, again depending on your policies. You can mention the account in a meeting, not pointing out the salesperson. You can repeat it in your one-on-one meetings letting them know they did a good job without putting them in the spotlight.

This goes back to what was discussed before. Treat everyone fairly, but not the same. You want to make sure everybody on the sales team understands you do see when they do well. You don't want to celebrate it too much to cause them to stop working, just enough to make them want the recognition again.

Now I will say, there are some companies which have policies which don't let you put anything in writing, "Just in case we need to terminate them." I understand why some companies do this. They may have had a lawsuit for firing someone. But the reason why this happens is because a lot of "managers" don't document their interactions with employees properly.

I've had no problems celebrating my team because when they did do something wrong, I also documented it properly. A lot of my career has been in California, where the state sides with the employee first. So, I've learned how to document any time there has been disciplinary issues. I also understood how, when, and where to take disciplinary actions.

Again, this may vary from state to state, so check with the laws in your state. I am not a lawyer and this is not legal advice! I know this has worked for me. I'm not going to go into all of the details on how to do this, what to say, etc. I'm keeping this at a higher level and will always refer you to your legal council.

Here's the overview. Talk to them first. Do not yell at a team member on the sales floor, talk to them in private. If this doesn't correct it, have a meeting, you may want to have someone else, i.e. a person from HR or other executive in it. Write it up with what needs to change and a timeline for corrective action. Have everyone sign and date the document. If at the end of that timeline, the changes have not happened, then you can terminate their employment. Hopefully, you'll be able to correct any issues before it gets to this point. Again, this is a guide and NOT legal advice. Before doing anything of this nature, talk to your lawyer.

The main points to remember is to celebrate in public, if not identifying the person directly, celebrate the account. If you hired the right people, gave them the best tools and coaching and have a great product or service, you should be doing more celebrating than disciplining. Remember, celebrate in public, discipline in private.

CHAPTER 13

Metrics: What Do You Watch and Measure?

Here's another area most business owners, managers, and executives completely miss and get wrong. What do you measure? Did you make forty calls today? Did you do ten presentations this week? Did you connect with fifty people this week? How much time did you spend on each call? How long was each meeting? What was covered on each call, in each meeting? What are you asking your sales team to do?

In my first job at a weekly newspaper, we were expected to make forty sales calls a day. That was how they measured us. As technology came to be, then they measured how long the calls were. They wanted to know how many presentations you did and how long were they. They checked how many people you spoke within any given day, week, month, etc. They were all looking at the wrong things.

My sales teams always knew I only checked one thing. How much did you bring in, today, this week, this month, this quarter? When I talk with business owners that start asking how many calls do I expect or meetings they should have, I stop them immediately. I ask them what they want. What matters to you?

I then ask, if everyone makes forty calls every day for the whole month, yet no new sales come in, are you going to be happy? Of course, they say no. Well then, why are you focusing on that? If they are able to do eighty presentations every month and no new sales come in, are you good? Again, no. Well then, what does it matter if they do eighty presentations or one? What is it you want? "I want sales." Then that's what we'll ask your sales team for, sales!

I know there have been many books written on metrics and I know many studies have shown it's a numbers game. And yes, when you call one-hundred people, you are bound to get a few at least. But it seems like an awful lot of work to get minimal results.

Why not focus on the results? When you tell a salesperson they need to close two new accounts per day, per week, per month, depending on your sales cycle, guess what happens. They do what they need to do to get those two sales. That is if they are good salespeople with good support.

When you set the expectations based on the end results, everyone involved in the sales process, VPs, directors, managers, coaches, etc., will do what they need to do to get the results. When you dumb down the results into metrics because you think you have a bunch of dumb salespeople, guess what you get? A dumb sales team.

When you set expectations on results and get them to tell you what they need to get there, guess what happens. First, you find out if you have the right people in place on all levels. Second, you'll find smart, successful, confident salespeople, who know what they need to do and what you want accomplished.

There have been several times in my career where people thought I was damn good at what I did because my team got results. I'll tell you a secret. It wasn't me. I set expectations, gave support, and let my team do their thing. I set expectations and held them accountable.

Occasionally, a salesperson would miss and I would coach them up and give them the tools they needed. If they wanted to be there, they hit it next time. But it wasn't me who did it. It was all of the great salespeople I had the privilege of working with. When you measure the results, that is what you get, results.

Doesn't that make sense? Common sense? Measure results and focus on effort when results aren't achieved.

CHAPTER 14

How to Pay Your Sales Team

This can be a tricky subject. There are a few different models, some used more successfully than others. I liked some commission built into my pay as I went through my sales career. I knew if I wanted a raise, I can just sell more. But not everyone is like me.

I have seen companies offer a straight commission. The salespeople only get paid on what they bring in. This sounds good, especially to small businesses or startups. But beware, if you use this model, you are telling the salesperson, you are not investing in them, so why should they invest in you? If they have a hard time hitting their stride or they are not bringing any accounts with them, this can make you burn through a lot of salespeople, putting more of a demand on the person training and coaching them. If there is a lot of turn over, they get burnt out training people because it's just a rotating door.

Some companies have a draw vs. commission. This means the salesperson gets some money to get by while they get up to speed. They have to pay back the money they took on the draw. Again, only a little risk on the employer side, but what happens if the person can't get to a point to pay back all of the money. You can put a cap on the draw, but again, when the salesperson hits the cap, they have no money coming in.

I have seen where a company pays a salary only. They show the salesperson they are investing in them. The problem is with this model does not motivate the salesperson to sell. They don't get any more if they sell or if they don't. Yes, you hired a good person and they will work hard, but it doesn't matter if they bring in one new client. They get paid the same.

Now I'm not saying those models can't work. They have worked for some companies, although I don't think they are the best model. I think the best is a blend of the first and last model. This is when the salespeople get a base salary, plus a commission structure. The base salary is not high. It's enough to get their bills paid. It's enough to cover their living expenses. If then they want more money, to go on vacation, to buy a new car, to buy a new house, they need to sell.

What the base is may depend on the market in which they live, the sales cycle, and the industry you are in, still it shouldn't be so big, that they are "too comfortable". You want your salespeople to understand you have skin in the game too and you are investing in them. If they are comfortable with the base then you have one of two problems. One, the base is too high. Two, they are not the salespeople you want.

The commission can be structured in a couple of ways. You can have a flat commission, i.e. 5% on all sales. You can have an upward sliding commission, meaning as you sell more, you get more commission. For example, for everything sold under $10,000 you get 3%, once you are over 10,000 it goes to 4%, at 25,000 it goes to 5%, etc. You can make it cover the total sales or it can apply to levels achieved. Again, following the example, if a salesperson sells $30,000, the first 10,000 gets 3%, the part between 10,001 and 25,000 gets 4% and everything over 25,001 gets 5%. That model can be hard on your accounting team, so keep them in mind.

You can also have a reverse sliding scale, where everything you sell up to 10,000 gets 5%, $10,001 to $25,000 gets 4% and everything over $25,001 gets 3%. I'm not a big fan of the last model because it can cause salespeople not to sell past a certain amount. You have to figure out what works for your business, in your industry and will attract the types of salespeople you want. I believe for most small businesses in most industries, the base with a flat or an upward sliding commission scale works the best.

How do you determine what works best for you? Talk to your salespeople about your current model. Talk to your accounting department to see what works with your business model. Look at your competition and see what they are doing. Then go and talk to salespeople you would love to hire and see how they are getting paid.

The last thing I will leave you with regarding pay is this: do not change your pay structure in a way which pays your sales team less without enough prior notice to them. I've seen companies do this and have most of their sales team leave in the next month or two. I would advise to not do it at all if it will lower their pay unless you are paying them too much to begin with, i.e. they are straight salary. Even then, I would give them a way to earn as much, if not more than they are making. The common sense practice here - pay for the results you want.

CHAPTER 15

What Relationship Do You Have with Your Customers?

As someone who runs a business, what role do you play in your sales, the lifeblood of your business? You can hire someone to run the sales team, but are you still involved? You should be. To what level is up to you, but you should understand the sales process. You should know some of your biggest clients. You should have a basic understanding, or a foundation, of your sales.

If you aren't involved, when sales are down, you won't know why. You will have to take the person running the sales team's opinion. They can give you all types of excuses and you won't really know what is going on. Do you think this is wise? The lifeblood of your business, the thing which keeps your business going and helps your business grow is a mystery to you. Does it sound like good business? That doesn't sound like common sense.

I'm not saying you have to run your sales team. I'd even say you shouldn't. But you should know the sales process. You should know who your biggest clients are. You should know your value proposition. If you don't, how do you communicate it to everyone else at the business? I know you wear a lot of hats, so having a basic understanding, a foundation of sales, is important. Hopefully, you are almost there now.

The sales process, we have already discussed, so you should be able to see when salespeople are getting stuck at certain stages. You should know where the training needs to be applied. You will know when you need to tweak the process, even if you don't do the tweaking. If you don't understand it, you won't know when it's working, and when it's not.

Your client base. It's important to be able to talk to them. Your sales team should have the main relationship with them and manage them. As I said before, you should get to know some of them too. Go on sales visits a couple of times a year, so you have experience on the front lines. And if your best salesperson leaves, then you should be able to talk to your customers, letting them know you still care about their business.

This is important, I've seen what happens to a company when a salesperson leaves and they do not tell the clients. It can, and has, resulted in a loss of a lot of business. Tell your clients about the transition and how valuable their business is.. If you don't, what's keeping them with your company? Once you lose a client, it's twice as hard to get them back.

It goes back to your value proposition. Make sure you remind your clients of it regularly. You need to make sure everyone knows it and understands its value. When one person or salesperson talks about your company's value proposition, their voice can get lost in a crowd. So remember, when the whole company says it, when the whole company values it, then the message becomes a roar in your industry. Make your business ROAR!

Even if you only want to play a minimal part in your sales, you should at least do these three things to ensure you have the foundation your business needs, know your value proposition, understand the sales process, and establish clear lines of communication. If you know these three things, you can bring others in to run the sales team, still, the foundation is there when something goes wrong. Not only will you have the skill set to make sure the business doesn't fail, you will have the skills to help your business survive, thrive, and grow.

CHAPTER 16

How to Run a Sales Meeting

This is another one of my pet peeves, sales meetings. They can be such a waste of time, energy and morale. Or they can be inspiring, motivating and uplifting. Which one do you want?

When I was at the glove manufacturing company, at one of my first sales meetings, the COO asked if she could sit in. Of course, I said yes. Really, was I going to say no to the COO? I wasn't worried or nervous. By this time, I have been holding sales meetings for over ten years. I knew what to do or rather, I knew what I did to make them effective.

The sales meeting started. I briefly went over the numbers for the last month. We were well short of where we needed to be. (I just started with the company and hadn't made changes yet.) I asked how many new companies learned about our gloves last month?

The sales guys I had at the time weren't too motivated. Before I got there, they would pick up faxes that came in, walk into the CEO's office and say, "Look what I just sold!" The CEO not knowing they never spoke with the person who faxed in the order, would say, "Good job!"

Now, that was not happening anymore. They knew I expected them to make calls to generate sales. The first sales guy said, "When are we going to get the gloves on back order?" I said it looks like a month, in the meantime we have other gloves to sell. He went on saying, "Yeah, but those are the ones I sell best. Why are they back ordered?" I told him, if we needed to have a separate meeting about that, we could set it up and to remind me after the meeting. Then I said, "How many new stores are in your pipeline to call?" He gave me a blank stare.

I said to the next sales guy, "Hey, I saw you closed that one big deal with the new store. Great job. Tell us how you found it and how you were able to get it going." He was excited and walked us through what he did and said. At the end, I again congratulated him and asked if anyone else thought they could do that. It didn't sound too hard. Everyone got a little excited and said yes, they could.

The first guy then asked, "When are we going to get new marketing materials for the gloves?" I said, "I don't know, if you want to talk about it further, we can set up a meeting. Remind me after this."

I then said to another sales guy, "We have a new master distributor in your old area, can you get with the Master's Team and walk through the numbers that are now their responsibility?" He said yes. I then went on to say, "Aren't you happy you no longer have to deal with the area. It was a hard one, right?" He shook his head yes and smiled. I continued, "Let me know what area you want next. Since you did so well with that monster of an area. I'll let you take a pick from the house territories." He got excited.

The first guy then chimed in, "What's going to happen when we have enough master accounts to cover all of their areas?" I said, "It will be a long time before that happens." He started in with "But-" which I quickly cut off with, "If you want to talk more about it, let's set up another meeting to talk about it. Remind me after this." I asked if anyone had any other topics directly related to selling. No one did. We ended the meeting.

The COO grabbed me after everyone was gone. She said, "Wow, I have never seen a sales meeting run so efficiently. And everyone seemed more excited, except for the first sales guy." I explained he always tries to distract from everyone feeling good and gaining momentum. He always wants to give reasons why he can't sell. I don't bite on it and always say we can set up another meeting to discuss his concerns.

Then I said, "You notice he did not stay behind to set up those meetings?" She said she had never seen that before and I took it as a high compliment.

Here's why it worked; his first question was directly related to sales, it was a backorder issue and I answered it. Then when he tried to drag it on more, I ended it. The next question had an indirect effect on sales, marketing materials. However, these were inside sales guys, they rarely sent those materials. It was a distraction, so I moved on. The last, was a concern which would affect their jobs down the line. It was so far in the distance - five to ten years - it wasn't worth talking about now. So again, I ended it.

I focused on the people who did a good job. The new sale the one guy had and the crappy territory the other guy no longer had to deal with and rewarded him for his efforts with his pick of a new territory. Everyone saw when they did a good job it was recognized and rewarded. Those people left excited. The one who did not, didn't have his job too much longer.

One of the biggest mistakes I see in sales meetings is managers going through policies and procedures. This is a HUGE mistake. They need to be covered but not at sales meetings. You set up separate meetings for those topics. Why?

Ok, here's where I get brutally honest. Those meetings are usually boring and unmotivating. I have never seen someone walk out of a meeting that covered policies and procedures with big smiles and ready to take on whatever came their way. They did not walk out saying, "Wow, now I know how to enter that order properly. This is a game-changer!!"

If you want to kill a day for salespeople, have a policies and procedures meeting at 8 am. I know, I know, they need to happen, so send a memo to the team first, explaining the new way, or reinforcing the old policy. Then have a short meeting, any time other than the first thing in the morning, asking if everyone understands it or has any questions. That's the best way to run those meetings and handle those situations. Let the managers have the long meetings to discuss it.

Sales meetings are for celebrating successes. Great job, you NAILED IT! It's for talking about new sales opportunities. You see how you can kill this one?

It's about motivation, getting salespeople excited, getting them ready to get out there and sell the hell out of what you got. Are you ready? It's exactly how you want people feeling leaving a sales meeting. So keep in mind, sales meetings should motivate.

If you feel like you get sales better now, then I am happy to help clarify. The next part is about the philosophy of life, personal, and business. I have worked with some businesses who had it covered, so if you skip this section, I fully understand and congratulate you. Or if you want to add more than just numbers to your business, something to make you want to get up every day and get after is, this next part will help you.

When everyone in your company understands this next part, I have seen how it helped companies grow and even, explode! If you want more than just a bricks and mortar business, more than just an e-commerce site, something adding to more than just a bottom line, then this next section will help you and your business as much as it's helped my career.

CHAPTER 17

Hapkido Creed:
Philosophy on Business and Life

When people meet me and start to talk to me, they are often surprised when they find out I'm a 4th degree black belt in Hapkido. I studied for ten years with Grandmaster Bong Soo Han and over ten years since his passing. I took a year off and studied Kali with Guru Danny Inosanto. I have been very fortunate to study with the incredible teachers I had.

What I learned on the mat, I have used more in business than on the street. To truly understand how you conduct business and especially sales, take a look at your philosophies. Are you just about the sale? Getting it at any cost?! Well, this is not what I am about.

And while I didn't realize it at the time, a lot of my philosophies came from my training in martial arts. Granted, I had a good upbringing. My mom did everything she could to provide food, clothing, and shelter, along with a basic understanding of right and wrong. You know the saying, 'do unto others as you'd have done to you.' It is what I was raised on. But when I got into my adult years, that's when I formed my business and life philosophies. That's when I found Hapkido or rather, it found me.

I started my career in sales at a weekly newspaper in Phoenix AZ, called New Times and I sold classified advertising. I'm aware I'm showing my age here as I worked at a newspaper when they still had and thrived on Classified Advertising.

Meanwhile, some of my friends and colleagues were training martial arts with one of the writers at the newspaper, Mike Kiefer. They all said I should join. I brushed it off. One evening at a happy hour, Mike was there and a few people again said I should train with them. I said I was fine and understood how to take care of myself.

That's when I heard Mike's voice behind me. As he grabbed one arm, he said, "What would you do if someone did this?" I quickly spun with my elbow out and stopped before it hit him in the head. "That's what I'd do," is what I replied. He asked me where I learned that. "On the street, the hard way," I replied, meaning I got beat up sometimes before learning. He explained Hapkido was about using natural movements to get around any threat and so I decided to give it a try.

I trained with Mr. Kiefer, who was a 3rd degree out of Chicago, for a year and a half before moving to Los Angeles to start a newspaper for New Times. On the mat, he was my teacher, so I refer to him as Mister Kiefer or Sir. Off the mat, he was my friend, so I called him Mike. When he found out I was going to Los Angeles, he said I needed to train with Bong Soo Han. He explained Bong Soo Han was the man who brought Hapkido to the US from Korea.

When I moved, I happened to live a mile down the road from Bong Soo Han's studio. Grand Master Han taught Hapkido is a way of life. So, I trained and learned the philosophies and the more I ran into challenges in my career, the more I found myself applying the Hapkido Creed to my professional life.

Courtesy: the showing of politeness in one's attitude and behavior toward others. Some may be surprised when I use courtesy and sales in the same sentence. Some think of sales in old-school ways, such as 'controlling the conversation' or 'influencing the decision'. Both of those techniques can be used in the right way when you are selling 6, 7, 8 figure products or services to C-Level executives and we've covered that. Even when using more sophisticated sales methods, courtesy is still critical.

In today's day and age of instant communication with technology being as advanced as it is, if you are rude, pushy, or what I consider unprofessional in any way, it gets out. Plus, do you want to be that person? Do you want to be rude and pushy? Do you want to be the annoying person everyone talks about until you walk in the room? If the room suddenly gets silent whenever you walk in, you may want to think about why this happens.

If you want to be courteous as a person and as a professional, you'll find you'll get further in business and in life. You've heard the expression, "You catch more flies with honey than with vinegar." It's true.

When I would call on a new prospect or talk to a new person I may do business with, I would always start with asking how they were. Then I wouldn't say anything until they answered. It made the person I was speaking with pay attention to me and the moment. If they were busy or it wasn't a good time to talk, I would reschedule. I was courteous of their time. Even when I was told no, I was courteous. It always paid off.

Integrity: the quality of being honest and having strong moral principles; moral uprightness. Now, I know some of you are questioning honesty in sales. Some may think you say anything you need to say to get the sale! Again, that doesn't work anymore. I don't think it ever really did.

One of my first "sales" jobs was selling vitamins over the phone. It was back before the internet when companies could do dishonest things and it didn't get out too fast. Calls would come into the call center. The calls were from people who got a notice saying they won one of these great prizes. Two were a trip to Hawaii and a new car! Wow, what a great deal, right? Ah, NO!

They would call in and we were supposed to sell them $900 worth of vitamins. The other prizes were books, certificates for food, and other things costing maybe $30-50. The vitamins' value? Maybe they were worth $80. It didn't take long for me to realize this was a scam. It was early in my career, before my Hapkido training, so I wasn't sure what to do. This was until I got a call from an elderly lady.

She called in and said she won. She was excited. I said yes you did, in order for me to see which prize she won, she had to buy the vitamins. She then told me her husband wasn't well, they were at the doctor a lot and the bills were adding up. I was going to hang up, until my manager, who was on the call with me, said, "Tell her, 'it sounds like you could really use the trip to Hawaii then.'" He sat over my shoulder, so I said that exactly. She said yes, it would and told me to hold on while she got her credit card.

My manager patted me on the shoulder and walked away. When she got back to the phone, I quickly said, "Ma'am, put your card away and don't respond to these types of mailings, they are all fake." Then I hung up.

The manager came back over and asked where the sale was. I said she changed her mind and I think I heard a voice in the background telling her to hang up. He then laid into me saying that I needed to learn how to push harder and not let her off the phone. So, I asked a question that really pissed him off, "How many trips and cars have been given out? So far, all I've heard people give away were the other garbage prizes."

Then he started yelling again, getting in my face, until I stood up. Yes, I was much taller and bigger than him. He took a couple of steps back and said, "Maybe this isn't for you. Not everyone has what it takes to succeed." I replied, very loudly so everyone in the room could hear, "Yes, I'm not good at conning people out of their money for crap prizes." I was about to continue and get into his face, when he quickly turned around, walked into his office and shut the door.

I collected my things and started to leave. A couple of people thanked me on the way out or gave me a thumbs up. I found out later, they were shut down about three months later. So even in those days before instant communication, word got around. Integrity mattered. Today, it doesn't take months for the truth to get around and to officials who will shut your business down.

You may question the people who said thanks or gave me a thumbs up, yet stayed there. I had a place to live and some money in savings. Some people don't have that. But I always repeat to those people, as the saying goes, "Do what you have to do, until you can do what you want to do." Keep the crappy job until you can find a better one. But you have to look for the better job and not just hope it falls in your lap. As business owners, you need to make sure what you offer and the people offering it have integrity. It has to have real value that your people explain properly.

Wisdom: the quality of having experience, knowledge, and good judgment; the quality of being wise. I'm not sure I agree with this definition with the exception of the good judgment part. I believe wisdom is the ability to use good judgment from the experience and knowledge you have. I know some people who are very knowledgeable but aren't wise. They know a lot, but don't know how to apply it properly.

I have run into that problem in business, in sales many times. When I was running a satire publication, The Onion, in Los Angeles, I was told I was going to be starting out with a salesperson who knew everything about The Onion and how to sell it. They were right about the first part, the salesperson knew a lot about the company, and yet it wasn't all he needed.

I went out on a few sales calls with him. He rattled off everything about what we had, the comedy people loved which was geared to a higher educated people with excess money to spend. We had great entertainment writers who got stories before anyone else or wrote reviews which were spot on. When we left, the prospect knew everything about the paper and our audience. Sound good? No! We walked away empty-handed.

This happened on another sales call, after which I sat down with him and asked him how he thought the calls went. He said he thought they were good. They understood everything about The Onion. I then asked him, what were the problems each of those companies had. What did they need? He looked at me and said he didn't know. I told him this is why they didn't go well. He had all of this knowledge about us, and despite this he couldn't apply it to their needs because he didn't know what they needed.

He then started to ask questions, listen, and apply his knowledge to their needs. He started closing more sales and building better relationships with the clients because the communication was a two-way street. He became a much wiser salesperson and person in general.

Perseverance: persistence in doing something despite difficulty or delay in achieving success. This is one of the most important characteristics I think every business and person needs to have. And just to be clear, it doesn't mean doing the same thing over and over and getting the same results. We all know that definition. It means continuing towards your goal, by different means if needed.

You may have heard a different version of this, success is in the follow-up. I know first-hand, this statement couldn't be more true. Does it mean you're going to get every person you talk to buying what you have? No. Why? Because not everyone you talk to will need what you have. You don't want to work with them because if they don't need it, you shouldn't offer it. That goes back to integrity. Your salespeople need to understand this.

It means once you find someone who needs what your business offers, continue the conversation. A lot of this depends on the sales cycle, which can be shortened with the right sales process, which we've already covered. Just as you can as a business owner, salespeople can feel burnt out when they get 'no' a lot or things don't feel like they are making progress.

When you started your business, was it easy? Did people fall at your feet wanting to hear about everything you have and buy it? If so, you should share what you did, so you can become a multi-billionaire. If you're like everyone else who started a business, it was hard. You may have been told 'no' a lot or that you wouldn't succeed, but you pushed on.

So, remember this and tell your story about what made you push through and persevere, it will help others. When I talk to salespeople who are frustrated things are not going as fast as they wanted, I always share the time I worked with an insurance inspection company.

I got lucky when I started and had a few companies wanting to work with us. They were smaller companies who didn't do many inspections. I wanted to get the bigger ones, like AmTrust. But they didn't have time to talk to me. They always pushed me off. You want to know what made it more frustrating? I knew they needed what we had. I know what we had was better than what they were using.

I called for a couple of years, yes years, with no progress. Then something happened which gave me a leg up. They bought a company we were already doing business with. So, I called and said we could continue to do that business for them, since we already knew it. I got in. From there, we were able to grow our business and relationship with them.

If I would have stopped after three calls, five calls, one year, two years, we wouldn't have gotten the business. But by having perseverance, and patience, I got it. Will this happen every time, maybe not. Unless someone says, "I never want, will never want, to do business with you. Never call again!", I will continue to try to have a conversation with them. In all honesty, even if they say that, I'll keep checking to see if the person leaves, then start again. Perseverance!

Self-Control: the ability to control oneself, in particular, one's emotions and desires or the expression of them in one's behavior, especially in difficult situations. This is a characteristic which is more important today than ever before. I wrote an article on LinkedIn about the "Screaming Sales Manager". In it, I explain how you get more progress and success with your sales team, when you don't scream at them all of the time. I introduce the concept I mentioned earlier of celebrating in public, while disciplining in private.

This may sound easy, however, if you don't practice it daily, it is hard. It's even harder when you don't realize you aren't using self-control. I have a lacrosse buddy from college who went into the military after college. He did really well and was promoted many times and now is a colonel. We had dinner with his family one day.

After dinner, we started talking. At a point in his career, he worked in the civilian world, while still in the reserves. He was called into the HR department at one point. They loved the work he did, but he needed to understand he was no longer in the military and couldn't scream at his workers when they didn't do what he asked. They were not soldiers and it was not the way to motivate them. He said it took a while to understand it because a lot of his career involved that type of behavior.

Then he told me when it finally hit home, literally. He was at home with his wife and little kids. His wife asked the kids to pick up their toys. Then she asked again five minutes later. Then after a third request a little later, he got involved. He started to scream at his kids, asking them if they didn't hear their mom and they needed to do it now!

His wife, who was a strong woman, immediately grabbed him and pulled him into the other room. She calmly explained these were his CHILDREN and not soldiers. He could not speak to them that way. He saw her face and then looked through the door at his kids. It hit him and hit him hard. After that, he got it. He needed self-control. He developed and it helped at work and at home.

Indomitable Spirit: a spirit which cannot be subdued or overcome, as persons, will, or courage. This ties into perseverance and is what gives you the ability to persevere. The funny thing about this characteristic is it's easy to see in a business. Does everyone there believe in what they are doing? If their business checked the integrity box, then they should. I've seen a lot of businesses where the people didn't believe in or get what they did. Those are the places where people worked just to get a paycheck.

I've also worked at companies who believe in what they had and what they do. Those were the best companies to work with and help grow. I worked with a work glove manufacturing company. The founder was great! He had a ton of energy and built a product which changed the industry. He and his brother took sporting technology and built it into work gloves. His brother was an engineer, which really made it work. It was easy to see how good they were and the benefits of using them.

They grew fast and were able to get the money and people to grow. During those growth years, they had setbacks. The gloves were so popular they couldn't keep up with demands. Some of the people who started with them, got frustrated, and yet they stuck with the company because they believed in it. It would have been easy to go find something easier, not having customers yell at them because they haven't gotten their orders.

So why didn't the people leave? Why didn't the customers just use something else? Indomitable Spirit! They knew what they had was great and believed in it. The customers knew they sold fast and were profitable. We changed our communication with the customers and reset expectations on when they get the gloves. Then everything went smoothly and the company continued to grow.

Perfection of Character: To turn inward and focus on development of oneself. A lot of martial arts, that focus on development, include this. Many wouldn't think this is a characteristic of a business. It makes the difference between the businesses just getting by and the ones who thrive.

I will add one thing to help set the mindset of this part. Here is a saying I have, "Perfection is fleeting". As soon as you find a perfect way to do something, soon enough there will be a better way to do it. People who don't get this point, and it's not easy, will be happy with the status quo. My biggest pet peeve when I work with businesses is when I ask them why they do something, the response I get is, "That's the way we've always done it." It just kills me.

If you are building a house and while framing and hammering in nails, every third swing you hit your hand, would you continue to do it this way? Granted, the nail does go in, however, your hand is swollen every day. The problem is sometimes businesses don't immediately feel the pain of those swing and misses. Business is moving along and the nails are going in.

When I first worked with the insurance inspection company, a father, son company, the son always was coming up with other ways to do business. The dad was used to doing it the way he's done it for over forty years and sometimes didn't want to hear about the new ways. Working with the son, we were able to explain how it was better for the company. How some of his ideas would save the company money or make it easier to do so.

Once the father saw the benefits, he came around. We were able to grow the company over 400% over the eight years I worked with them. A lot of that came from constantly looking at how to improve what we did. You can look to create Perfection of Character for your business by looking internally at what you are doing.

Do any of these things happen overnight or instantly? No! I know in the age of instant gratification, working on areas of your business which takes a long time isn't fun. I know it's tempting to grab the quick money at any cost. Nevertheless, when you create this foundation, your business will have a longer life, people will want to do business with you, and your employees will want to continue to work there and help grow the business. What is your business creed? If you don't have one, please feel free to add the Hapkido Creed as your business creed and see how it helps.

CHAPTER 18

Conclusion

I'm sure you now have a better understanding of the "S" word - sales is the lifeblood of your business. I don't think any of it is too tough for anyone to follow or implement into their business. I have seen each of these ideas successfully used in business and believe they will help every small business or any business for that matter. This all should seem simple, but don't confuse simple for easy.

Did this teach you absolutely everything you need to know about sales, of course not! This did not go into techniques or sales methods because the purpose wasn't about the minor details of your process. With the foundation of sales you now have, you can understand your sales better and be able to talk to your sales team more effectively.

By now, you will have a good base to understand your sales. Can you learn more? Absolutely, if you want to learn more, you can go to my site and get access to further training. If you haven't already bought *The "S" Word Workbook*, I recommend you do now and start taking action on what you've learned from this book.

I purposely made the book and the workbook easy to follow. It's business. It's sales. It's common sense. And when common sense becomes common practice, that's when you'll find success.

Go be successful!

For information on further training:
LinkedIn: https://www.linkedin.com/in/robbedell/
Website: www.robbedell.com